PUBLISHING

Speaking in Sentences

Oral language activities to take the struggle out of literacy

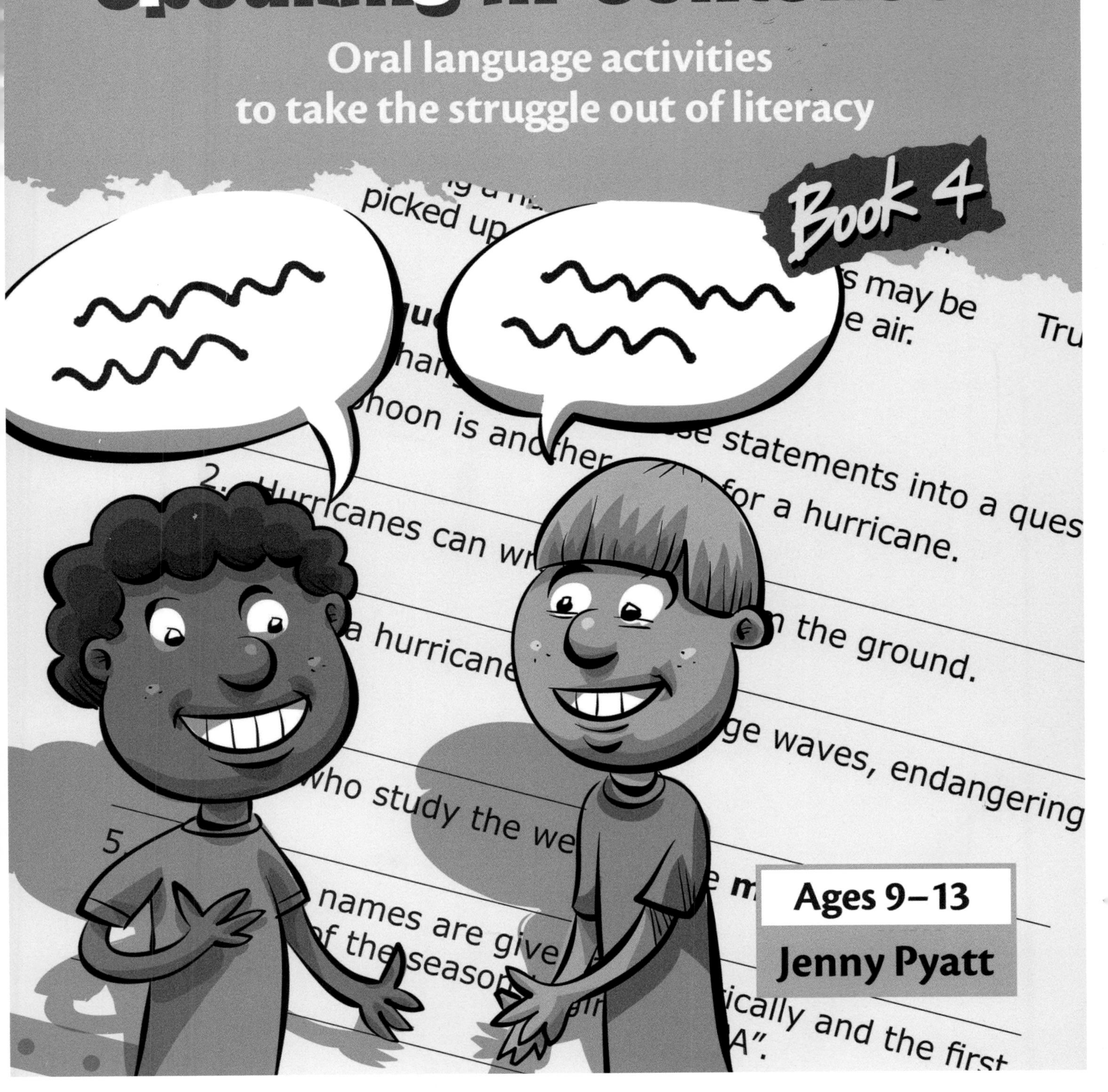

Book 4

Ages 9–13

Jenny Pyatt

Title: Speaking in Sentences Book 4 (Ages 9-13)

Author: Jenny Pyatt

Editor: Tanya Tremewan

Designer: Freshfields Graphic Design

Book code: PB00052

ISBN: 978-1-908735-36-2

Published: 2012

Publisher: TTS Group Ltd

Park Lane Business Park
Kirkby-in-Ashfield
Notts, NG17 9GU
Tel: 0800 318 686
Fax: 0800 137 525

Website: www.tts-shopping.com

About the author: Jenny Pyatt has a background of 27 years in teaching pupils from Years 1–8. She has a strong interest in helping those for whom English is a second language which stemmed from teaching experiences in East and South Auckland, New Zealand.

Now semi-retired and living on a lifestyle block in Hawke's Bay, Jenny spends her time writing, raising calves and tending a four-acre garden.

CONTENTS

INTRODUCTION

Speaking in Sentences is an asset-rich series with a user-friendly oral language programme that is both fun and interesting for you and for the children you teach. The activities in Book 4 are aimed at pupils for ages 9-13 and can also be adapted for younger children.

If you ask most teachers about their oral language programme in the classroom, they immediately think of the core components of plays, news, current events, poetry and speeches. The ideas in this book present these standard components in a range of different ways that will bring new life to them. You will also discover new ideas and suggestions for other ways of encouraging your children to speak confidently and clearly, to speak in full sentences and to use correct grammatical structures.

In addition, although not written specifically for teaching EAL pupils, this material would be an excellent supplement to any EAL programme.

This book is divided into two sections:

1. **Activities for the classroom** covers a diversity of activities that the classroom teacher can put to everyday use in the classroom programme.
2. **Intensives** focuses on ideas for teaching children who have special needs in regard to oral language.

On the final pages, you will also find a suggested one-year oral language programme for ages 6-13, which draws on all four books in the *Speaking in Sentences* series.

Not all the activities require formal assessment. Many can be used simply to build confidence when speaking in small and large groups. This greater confidence can then become a springboard for more formal situations such as making prepared speeches.

CURRICULUM LINKS

<table>
<tr><td colspan="2">Learning strand: 1. Speaking
Most children learn to:
• Speak competently and creatively for different purposes and audiences, reflecting on impact and response
• Explore, develop and sustain ideas through talk</td></tr>
<tr><td>Year 5
• Present a spoken argument, sequencing points logically, defending views with evidence and making use of persuasive language</td><td>Year 6
• Use a range of oral techniques to present persuasive arguments and engaging narratives
• Use the techniques of dialogic talk to explore ideas, topics or issues</td></tr>
<tr><td colspan="2">Year 6 progression into Year 7
• Use exploratory, hypothetical and speculative talk as a tool for clarifying ideas</td></tr>
<tr><td colspan="2">Learning strand: 2. Listening and responding
Most children learn to:
• Understand, recall and respond to speakers' implicit and explicit meanings
• Explain and respond to speakers' use of language</td></tr>
<tr><td>Year 5
• Analyse the use of persuasive language</td><td>Year 6
• Analyse and evaluate how speakers present points effectively through use of language and gesture</td></tr>
<tr><td colspan="2">Year 6 progression into Year 7
• Listen for and recall the main points of a talk, reading or TV programme, reflecting on what has been heard to ask searching questions, make comments or challenge views expressed
• Identify the main methods used by presenters to explain, persuade, amuse or argue a case</td></tr>
<tr><td colspan="2">Learning strand:3. Group discussion and interaction
Most children learn to:
• Participate in conversations, making appropriate contributions building on others' suggestions and responses</td></tr>
<tr><td>Year 5
• Understand different ways to take the lead and support others in groups
• Understand the process of decision making</td><td>Year 6
• Understand and use a variety of ways to criticise constructively and respond to criticism</td></tr>
<tr><td colspan="2">Year 6 progression into Year 7
• Adopt a range of roles in discussion
• Identify and report the main points emerging from discussion
• Acknowledge other people's views, justifying or modifying their own views in the light of what others say</td></tr>
</table>

Source: Adapted from the Primary Framework for Literacy and Mathematics 2006

Learning strand: 1. Listening and responding 1.1 Developing active listening skills and strategies 1.2 Understanding and responding to what speakers say in formal and informal contexts	
Year 7 • Identify key features of speech in a variety of contexts, and some key skills and strategies used by speakers	**Year 8** • Explain the effect of specific features of speech, the skills and strategies used by speakers, and identify areas for improvement
• Identify, sift and summarise the most important points or key ideas from a discussion	• Explain the speaker's intentions and make inferences from speech in a variety of contexts
Learning strand: 2. Speaking and presenting 2.1 Developing and adapting speaking skills and strategies in formal and informal contexts 2.2 Using and adapting the conventions and forms of spoken texts	
Year 7 • Tailor the structure and vocabulary of take to clarify ideas and guide the listener • Use some verbal techniques to make talk interesting for listeners	**Year 8** • Select the most appropriate way to structure speech for clarity and effect • Engage listeners' attention and interest by using a range of different verbal techniques
• Recognise different conventions and forms in speech	• Make appropriate selections from a range of conventions and forms in speech
Learning strand: 3. Group discussion and interaction 3.1 Developing and adapting discussion skills and strategies in formal and informal contexts	
Year 7 • Make clear and relevant contributions to group discussion	**Year 8** • Make a sustained contrition to group discussion, and illustrate and explain their ideas

Source: Adapted from The National Strategies: The Framework for Secondary English

SECTION ONE

Activities for the classroom

The ideas in this section offer a novel and engaging approach to your oral language programme.

A. Moving on from news

For many children when they start school, news is a significant part of the day. It is a valuable time for them to get off their chest any topic or experience that is so important to them on that particular morning. For some children, the first time that they share their news is a real sign that they are settling in and want to be a part of the class.

It might seem unusual, therefore, to be discussing news as an activity for pupils at this level. However, for a variety of reasons, some pupils at this age are still coming to school and having their daily news session.

News sessions can be a useful element in the oral language programme, as an opportunity to teach the skills of listening and questioning. Older children might have sports results to report to the class. Alternatively, a special holiday such as a trip overseas can be informative, create discussion, and be a learning opportunity for everyone.

Activity 1: **Doughnut news**

Doughut news is a great way to achieve maximum pupil participation. It is also a good way to use time on a Monday morning, when many children want to share something that has happened in the weekend.

Procedure

1. The children are seated in pairs in two concentric circles. The outer circle faces inwards and the inner circle faces outwards. Each child sits opposite their partner.
2. Give the pairs two minutes to share their news.
3. After two minutes, the inner circle stands and moves one space in a clockwise direction so that they have a new partner.
4. The new pairs have two minutes to share their news.
5. News sharing continues in this way until the time limit you set for this activity is up.

Activity 2: **Structured and diverse news session**

As the months go by, some children may still want to have news regularly but others may have moved on and become bored with the standard news session. This is a signal to give the news session more structure so that it caters for different abilities and needs. The following ideas will help you run this kind of session.

Procedure

- Have several oral language activities happening during the news session (which may already be the standard approach of small rural schools with composite classes). These activities will be an extension for some pupils and a part of the process of "moving on" to a more structured oral language lesson.
- Make all children aware of which day it will be their turn to have news, or to present their oral language activity.
- When you introduce the first structured activity, allocate it to a group of more confident and articulate pupils.
- Within a short period, in most classes, all children will want to try the new activities and "home news" can be limited to important events.

Hint

See Book 3 in the *Speaking in Sentences* series for oral language activities ("D. More reading aloud", "G. Television viewing" and "J. Bookselling" in Section One) that would be suitable to incorporate into news sessions.

B. Storytelling

Telling stories helps to teach children the skill of sequencing events. They use problem-solving skills as they plan how to tell the story. They build a strong vocabulary and develop their self-confidence.

Activity 1: **Introduction**

Procedure

1. Brainstorm the following questions as a class:
   - Why do people tell stories?
   - Can you remember people telling you stories when you were little?
   - Who told you stories when you were little?
   - What is the first story that you can remember hearing?
   - When do you think the first story was ever told? When did storytelling begin?
2. Give out a copy of the following template on ***a touch of history*** to each pupil and read it together as a class.

Read together.

A touch of history

Science tells us that, like the apes, our ancestors didn't talk but made sounds. As humans developed so did their speech. First there were words and then humans began to put words together to make sentences. People didn't travel very much so thousands of different languages and dialects developed in individual communities which had no great need to communicate with other communities.

In the beginning, people told simple stories around a campfire. Stories filled the need for entertainment, the need to communicate and to record actions. They filled a need for beauty and form, through language and music. Creating songs, poems and ballads gave pleasure. Folk stories were repeated by generation after generation. People used their imaginations to embellish the stories and make them more exciting. The stories might have been about encounters with animals, either real or imaginary. Early artists told stories by painting pictures on cave walls.

Storytellers emerged. Many good storytellers encouraged, inspired and guided people. But there were also storytellers who had more negative effects.

Much later, with the advent of radio, listeners continued to visualise their own mental pictures. Playwrights and film makers used costumes and other props to help create their stories.

Today, with television, the images are provided for us.

Activity 2: **Find a story**

Procedure

1. Give a copy of the ***instructions and planning*** template that follows to each child in the class. They use these planning sheets to find out about a story on their local area.
2. Because the emphasis is on oral language, the children must re-tell these stories to the class.
3. They write down their stories and perhaps create a wall display.

Extensions

- Make a time when children can share their local stories with another class. ("Did you know that ...?")
- Discuss whether the stories are fact or fiction.

Activity 3: **The story of my life**

Vocabulary	
biography	autobiography

Procedure

1. Discuss the vocabulary for this activity, clarifying the difference between a *biography* and an *autobiography*.
2. With the class seated in a circle, explain that everyone will be telling the story of their life so far – their family and where they grew up.
3. Be a role model for this activity by being the first one to give a brief summary of your life.
4. Pupils take it in turns to tell their life story. It may be an impromptu activity but they must try to keep their audience interested.

Extension

Children tell the life story of an object.

- Brainstorm this activity together. For example, finish this story on the whiteboard: *This book began as a tree growing in a forest ...*
- Children choose a paper clip, a slipper, a cup, a tree or any other object to tell their story about.
- Give them time to plan this presentation, perhaps as a homework exercise.

Instructions and planning sheet: **my area**

Research any local story about your area or town. For example, find out how the local streets or rivers were named. Are there any local myths or legends?

Ask your parents and grandparents for any stories about the district. Are there any haunted houses nearby? Are there mines or any other dangerous spots where accidents might have occurred? Where did people go in the old days for entertainment or old-fashioned dances?

Remember you are telling a story. You can use your imagination to make it more exciting.

You might begin with:

Once upon a time …

Many years ago …

Did you know that …

Now plan your story.

Our district

Activity 4: Story of a painting

In this activity, the class studies a painting and tells a story – either a narrative or a biography – about it.

Hint

A classical painting works well for this activity.

Procedure

1. As a class, revise the elements of a narrative: the setting, characters, plot, problem, solution or resolution.
2. Study a painting.
3. Brainstorm together a few possible sentences of a story.
4. Sit the class in a circle. Ask for a volunteer to give you the first sentence of the story. You may also want to choose one child to be the recorder.
5. Go around the circle with each child adding to the story.

Activity 5: An imaginary journey

The pupils' challenge is to tell the story of a journey.

Procedure

1. Give each child a copy of the ***instructions and planning sheet*** that follows.
2. Children work individually or in pairs to create the story of a journey. If they work in pairs, each child will need to tell a part of the story.
3. In pairs or individually, children tell their story to the rest of the class.
4. Use the *oral language assessment* template below to assess each child's contribution (or arrange for peer assessment).

Oral language assessment: telling a story

Task: Plan and tell a story of an imaginary journey

Name of pupil: ______________________ Date: ____________

Tick the box if you agree with the statement.

Content	*Tick if Yes*
The story was well sequenced.	☐
The story had a clear beginning, middle and ending.	☐
The speaker used a range of vocabulary.	☐
Presentation	
The speaker captured and held the attention of the audience.	☐
The speaker used good expression.	☐
The speaker used appropriate volume and speed.	☐
The speaker's stance was relaxed but confident.	☐
The speaker used gestures effectively.	☐

Instructions and planning sheet

1. Your task is to tell the story of an imaginary journey.You could use one of the "Suggested topics" below or use one of your own ideas for an imaginary journey.
2. Use the "My plans" space below to plan your journey. Make brief notes or create a diagram with arrows to use as a cue card.
3. Practise telling your story.
4. Present your imaginary journey to the class.

Suggested topics

The journey to stardom
A treasure hunt
Rafting down a river
A journey into space
A ball bounced out of my hands, down the hill ... where did it go?
Through a black hole
Looking through a window

My plans

Activity 6: **Using miscellaneous objects to create a story**

This is the first of two activities that use a variety of objects as the inspiration for developing a story. In this activity, you work together as a class.

Procedure

1. Gather together a container full of objects (eg, classroom items such as a pencil, a book, a stapler).
2. Hold the container above pupils' eye level and ask four children to select one object each from the container.
3. The class creates a story around the four items that have been chosen.

Hint

Leftover treasures from Christmas crackers are great as objects for this activity.

Extension

- Take the same four objects to a neighbouring class. This class creates its own story using the same four objects.
- Share the different stories in assembly.

Activity 7: **Using miscellaneous objects to solve a mystery**

This second activity based on miscellaneous objects is designed for small group work.

Procedure

1. Gather together some miscellaneous objects. Divide them into groups of six unrelated objects and put each group in a separate envelope. You may need up to 10 envelopes, depending on the size of your class.
2. Tell the class that a crime has been committed – a murder or theft.
3. Divide the class into groups of three to four, and give each group one envelope. The envelope contains the evidence about the crime. The group builds a story around these items.
4. Each group reports to the class. It states the crime that was committed, reveals the evidence and states its case.

Activity 8: ***What if* stories**

Here is an activity that draws heavily on the imagination to develop oral language skills.

Procedure

1. As a class, discuss some "what if" questions such as:

   What if everything in the world was purple?

   What if everything you touched turned to gold?

   What if all people had four legs?
2. Ask the children to suggest some "what if" ideas of their own.
3. Use this activity to spark some impromptu speeches.

Activity 9: **Story grids**

A story grid offers vocabulary to prompt ideas and suggest a loose structure for a story.

Procedure

1. Organise children into pairs and give each pair a copy of a story grid template that follows (any one from ***Grid One*** to ***Grid Six***).
2. In their pairs, the children work out a story using all the words on the grid. They practise the story. Each child must tell a part of the story. In the meantime, you move around the class listening and making suggestions when the children are stuck.
3. Each pair joins up with another pair and the two pairs exchange their stories.
4. Give a copy of the ***Grid Seven*** template (a blank grid) to every child. Each child thinks of a topic and writes 12 words associated with it on the grid. Then either:
   - the child swaps grids with a friend and each of them tells a story using the words on the grid, or
   - you collect the grids and use them as topics for impromptu speeches (see *Speaking in Sentences*, Book 1, page 13).
5. For assessment of speeches forthcoming from the story grids, use the ***peer assessment*** template that follows.

Name of speaker: ______________________ Date: ____________

Story grid number: ☐ Assessed by: ________________

Tick the box if you agree with the statement.

Content	*Tick if Yes*
The speaker linked the words together well.	☐
The story was well sequenced.	☐
The story was interesting.	☐
Delivery	
The speaker's voice was clear.	☐
The speaker held eye contact with the audience.	☐
The speaker used appropriate volume.	☐
The speaker spoke at good pace – not too fast and not too slow.	☐

Grid One

summer	Josh	beach	shark
frightened	surfers	screamed	swimming
flags	teeth	sandcastle	help

Grid Two

mobile phone	new	birthday	school
classroom	rules	friend	teacher
lost	trouble	party	Sophie

Grid Three

frog	tadpole	swimming pool	egg
fish	fly	fishing rod	pond
drowned	sunny	running	happy

Grid Four

egg	leaf	chrysalis	coloured
fluttered	butterfly	garden	crawled
munching	caterpillar	school	playground

Grid Five

Tyrannosaurus rex	extinct	ago	dinosaur
flew	leaf eater	swam	heavy
walked	died	grass	people

Grid Six

skiing	snow	avalanche	slid
mountain	searched	worried	relief
sledge	uninjured	ambulance	ski-patrol

Grid Seven

C. Listening and responding to texts I: coal

This is the first of four topics, with a set of related activities, that involve listening and responding to texts. You can use each topic as part of a curriculum study, or as a general knowledge component of your oral language programme.

This first topic deals with coal. Work with this topic for one or two weeks.

Activity 1: **Dictagloss**

This first activity gets pupils interacting with and processing information about coal.

Procedure

1. The children find a partner.
2. Tell the children, "You are going to listen to a text. You need to focus on the key ideas and try to remember all the important points. You need to remember them because you are going to retell the text to your partner."
3. Read ***Text One*** out loud twice. As you are reading the text for the second time, write some key words on the whiteboard.
4. One child in each pair retells the text to their partner.
5. The storytelling pupil asks, "Can you think of anything else?" and their listening partner then attempts to fill in any gaps.
6. The whole class tries to retell the text. Write the class version on the whiteboard and compare it to the original. Are all the main ideas there?
7. Read ***Text Two***, with each pair of children reversing the roles of storyteller and listener.
8. Continue working through the texts in this way, with pupils finding a new partner after every second text.

Hint

It is important to begin with short texts of just a few sentences, then to gradually increase the length and complexity of the text. The order of the texts here reflects this gradual build-up.

Extensions

- Pupils mark the main coal mining areas on a map of the UK, including the date(s) when the mining was at its height in each area.
- Pupils build a list of mining vocabulary from the texts and do research on the history related to the words that interest them most. They present a brief report on their findings to the class.

Text One: About coal

Coal is a solid, rock-like substance. It is called a fossil fuel because it comes from fossilised plants and other once-living materials. Over millions of years, geological pressures and processes turned this dead matter first into peat and later into different grades of coal, from brown lignite to glossy black anthracite.

Text Two: Uses of coal

Over the centuries, coal has been used in many ways. Often it has been burnt to cook or keep warm. In addition, jet, which is a form of lignite coal, has been used as an ornamental stone since the Iron Age and is still sometimes polished. Most coal now is used to provide energy to make electricity. It is also used in various ways in heavy industry, such as in making plastics, tar, synthetic fibres, fertilisers, medicines and steel.

Text Three: When coal was first used.

Coal has been used by people for thousands of years. In 2005 a coalstone hunting camp from the Stone Age – about 120,000 years ago – was discovered in Germany. There coal was used for campfire cooking. The Chinese people have been mining coalstone for fuel for 10,000 years. Coal was used for funeral pyres in Britain during the Bronze Age (2000–3000 years BC). It was commonly used in the early period of the Roman occupation but did not have great importance in Britain until after about 1000 AD. Around 1800, the Industrial Revolution led to the large-scale use of coal to fuel steam engines.

Text Four: Early mines

First supplies of coal were found lying on the surface of the ground. Drift mining – cutting into the side of the earth rather than tunnelling straight downwards – probably came next. Drift mines from medieval period have been found in the Forest of Dean. Later, small-scale shaft mines were used. To work a bell pit mine, a shaft was dug down to reach the coal. The coal was then taken out by bucket. No supports were used. Mining continued until the mine collapsed or became too dangerous. A bell pit mine is shaped like an upturned bell. Room and pillar mines were underground mines where rooms of coal were dug out with pillars left to support the roofs. As a result, quite a lot of usable coals was left behind.

Text Five: Mining today

In some places, surface mining is still a way of extracting coal. But mining technology now allows improved methods for both surface and underground mining. Everything is done on a much larger scale and uses more and bigger machinery.

As demand for coal became greater and greater during the Industrial Revolution, underground mines became deeper and deeper. The deeper the mines went, the more difficult and dangerous the work became.

Over the years, heavy machinery has been increasingly used in the mining process. Machines have gradually replaced many manual labourers. Technological developments during the 19th and 20th centuries also helped to improve both the safety of miners and the output of mines. Modern mining methods now allow us to easily reach most of our coal reserves. The amount of coal produced by one miner in one hour has more then tripled since 1978.

Text Six: Mining problems

Safety has always been a big issue for mine workers. It can be a very dangerous job. The main risks are mines collapsing, explosions caused by the gases that are trapped underground, flooding of mine shafts, rock falls, falling down shafts or being run over by coal carts or other machinery. The worst single disaster in British coal mining history was at Senghenydd in South Wales. On the morning of 14 October 1913 an explosion and the fire that followed killed 436 men and boys.

The other major problem that can come from mining is damage to the environment. When coal is exposed to water and air, sulphuric acid can form. As water drains from the mine, the acid moves into waterways. Rain falling on the mine tailings (the waste material from the mine) can also produce the acid, whether the mine is still operating or not. Sulphuric acid can leave soil infertile and pollute streams, killing plants, fish and other aquatic animals. Burning coal also gives off carbon dioxide into the air. An excess of carbon dioxide is linked with global warming.

Activity 2: **Hotseating**

This activity is an opportunity for pupils to draw on their growing knowledge of the topic while developing their interviewing skills.

Procedure

1. Read out the ***further information*** text that follows.
2. Ask for a volunteer to sit in the hotseat and take the role of a coalminer. The rest of the class are journalists interviewing this coalminer about his or her day.
2. Ask for a volunteer to sit in the hotseat and take the role of the son/daughter of a coalminer. Again, the rest of the class are journalists, asking about what this child does in leisure time, and how this child helps his or her parents.

Further information

Throughout the 19th and 20th centuries, coalfields helped to create prosperity in Lancashire, Yorkshire and South Wales. The Yorkshire pits that supplied Sheffield were only about 300 feet deep. Northumberland and Durham were the leading coal producers and they were the sites of the first deep pits. Some were over 1000 feet deep.

Activity 3: **From statement to question**

Pupils' experience of "journalism" through Activity 2 will develop their questioning abilities. This activity gets them to focus specifically on the skill of making questions.

Procedure

1. Give a copy of the ***making questions*** template that follows to each child in the class.
2. Children complete the template individually.

Activity 4: **Three–two–one**

The aim of this activity is to develop confidence and fluency in relation to the topics of life in the coalmines.

Procedure

1. Organise pupils into pairs.
2. One child in each pair has three minutes to speak to his or her partner on the topic of "Life in the coalmine".
3. After three minutes, call out "Stop!" and then the second child starts to speak for three minutes on one of these topics.
4. After your second call of "Stop!", children find a new partner. This time each pupil in the pair has two minutes to speak.
5. By now the children are becoming more confident. For the third and final time, they find a new partner and speak on their topic for just one minute.

Making questions

The following sentences are statements. Can you turn each statement into a question?

1. Coal can be used for making jewellery and ornaments.

____

____

2. Coal was first used for hunters' campfires.

____

____

3. Collecting coal close to the surface was called drift mining.

____

____

4. Room and pillar mines were underground mines where rooms of coal were dug out with pillars left to support the roofs.

____

____

5. Mines collapsing and gas explosions are two of the main dangers of coal mining.

____

____

6. When coal is exposed to water and air, sulphuric acid can form, which can drain from the mine and into waterways.

____

____

D. Listening and responding to texts II: survival in the desert

This is another set of activities that you can use as part of a curriculum study, or as a general knowledge component of your oral language programme. This topic deals with the challenges that living things face in the desert and how they manage to survive there. Work with this topic for one or two weeks.

Activity 1: **Introduction**

Procedure

1. As a class, brainstorm these questions:
   - What is a desert?
   - What are the characteristics of a desert?
   - Where are the world's deserts?
   - What is an oasis?
2. Give out a copy of the ***background information*** that follows to each pupil and read through the information together.
3. Children complete the map activity (also on the ***background information*** template) independently.

Activity 2: **Dictagloss**

This activity makes use of short texts to develop pupils' listening skills.

Procedure

Working with the following texts (***Text One*** to ***Text Four***), use the same procedure as for Activity 1 in Part C above.

Activity 3: **Research**

This activity gets pupils working independently to discover more about life for an animal in the desert.

Procedure

- Pupils choose a partner to work with.
- As their research topic, the pair chooses an animal that can live in the desert. They go to the library and find **three facts** about this animal.
- As a class, the children share their information and make a classroom display about animals that have adapted to life in the desert.

Extension

- Each pair develops a dialogue about life in the desert. The two characters in the dialogue are their chosen animal.

Read together.

Background information about deserts

Deserts occur in areas where evaporation greatly exceeds rainfall. More than one-fifth of the Earth's surface is classified as desert.

In a desert there is hardly any water. During the day, the sand and rocks are burning hot to touch but at night the desert can be freezing cold. The Gobi Desert is always cold. Few plants are able to grow in a desert but many different animals still manage to survive in these conditions. Most of the animals are nocturnal. Hiding during the day helps them to avoid the heat. Spadefoot toads spend nine months of the year underground.

Most animals live on the edge of the desert or around oases.

On the map below, draw the **Sahara Desert** in Africa, the **Great American Desert** (also known as Death Valley), the **Gobi Desert** in Asia and the **deserts of central Australia**. Use an atlas to help you.

Text One: Dromedary

The Sahara Desert is in Africa. It is the biggest desert in the world. The dromedary camel lives here. It is used to carry heavy loads. It has one hump that is full of fat. This camel can use the fat for energy instead of eating food. It has long shaggy hair that traps a layer of cool air against its skin so that it hardly ever sweats and its long eyelashes help to keep the sand out of its eyes.

Text Two: Oryx

White oryx are a kind of antelope that live in the Sahara Desert. They live together in small herds. They have long horns. Looking at them from one side you can see only one horn. Could this be a unicorn?

Text Three: Cactus

Cacti live in hot locations like the Great American Desert, which is actually the hottest place on Earth. It only rains here twice a year but some plants survive. Cacti store water in their fleshy leaves. Their spines protect the leaves from animals that want to drink the water.

Text Four: Kangaroo

Some marsupials live in the Australian deserts. A marsupial keeps its babies in a pouch where they grow and feed. The red kangaroo is the biggest marsupial. Its heavy, powerful tail gives balance and stability. Kangaroos keep cool by licking saliva over their face. They mainly graze on grass.

Behaviour: Play fighting is common among young kangaroos and between the mother and her young. They grasp each other around the neck, touch forepaws and kick.

E. Listening and responding to texts III: natural disasters

Used as part of a curriculum study, or as a general knowledge component of your oral language programme, this topic gets pupils learning and thinking about:

- natural disasters in general (Activities 1, 10, 12)
- droughts and floods (Activities 2–4)
- extreme winds (Activities 5–8)
- earthquakes (Activity 9)
- volcanic eruptions (Activity 11)

Work with this topic for one or two weeks.

Activity 1: Introduction

Vocabulary		
disaster	drought	flood
anticyclone	moisture	earthquake
tsunami	hurricane	cyclone
landslide	volcanic eruptions	avalanche

Procedure

1. As a class, discuss: What is a natural disaster? Brainstorm for the different kinds of natural disasters and list them on the whiteboard.
2. Beside each natural disaster on the list, note its immediate effect on the people and animals that have been living in the place where it strikes.
3. For homework, pupils find out about a natural disaster that has struck somewhere around the world and prepare a report to present to the class.

Activity 2: Introducing droughts and floods

Procedure

1. List these words on the whiteboard and ask the children to copy them: *drought, flood, moisture, anticyclone, thunderstorm, rain.*
2. To encourage them to focus, tell the children you will read them some information and they should tick off each word on their list as you say it.
3. Read the ***background information*** that follows.

Activity 3: Droughts and floods – dictagloss

Procedure

Working with ***Text One*** and ***Text Two*** that follow, use the same procedure as for Activity 1 in Part C above.

Background information

Long periods without rain are known as **droughts**. During a drought, moisture on the ground evaporates. The ground dries out, cracks and hardens or turns to dust. Shallow-rooted plants cannot reach the moisture in the soil and die. Animals that graze on grass have no food.

Floods occur when there is so much water in a river that it overflows on to the land and through houses. Flooding usually happens after several weeks of steady rain or when thunderstorms produce large volumes of water in a short time. Conditions that encourage flooding are lots of rain combined with high tides, or melting snow in spring when the earth is partly frozen and doesn't absorb the overflowing water from the rivers. In a big flood, people can drown; houses, cars and trees are swept away.

Text One: Living by the sea

Many people like to live beside the sea. As the moon travels around the Earth, it causes two high tides each day. People who live beside the sea are at risk from the tides. Occasionally spring tides rise much higher than normal. Spring tides can cause floods through homes that are on flat land near the sea.

Text Two: After a flood

After a flood there is loads of cleaning up to do. The water has gone but has left behind mud and silt through the houses. Carpets and furniture are soaked. There may be no electricity to help dry things out. Everything smells.

Bridges have been washed out and food is slow in coming to the flooded area. When it comes, it may be different food and not what people are used to.

Activity 4: **Droughts and floods – strategies for note taking**

This activity helps pupils develop their note-taking skills by encouraging them to look for the main ideas in a text.

Procedure

1. Give each child a copy of the ***background information*** introduced in Activity 2 above.
2. As a class, discuss the main ideas of text and highlight or underline them.

Activity 5: **Introducing extreme winds**

This activity introduces the subtopic of extreme winds: hurricanes and tornadoes.

Procedure

1. Read the background information on ***air movement*** below to the class.
2. Give out a copy of the ***activity sheet*** that follows to each pupil.
3. Discuss each *true or false*? statement as a class, then pupils circle the answers.
4. Pupils complete the *making questions* activity on their own.

Air movement: **a simple explanation**

In warm weather, land warms up more quickly than the sea. In cold weather the land becomes cold more quickly than the sea. In summer, as the land warms up, the warm air rises and a sea-breeze blows on to the land to replace the warm air as it rises. At night, the land cools down quickly while the air above the sea is warmer, so wind moves off the land to replace the air that is rising off the sea. This air movement is more extreme over oceans.

Most of us have sat inside and listened to a thunderstorm raging around the house. Sometimes we have watched the hailstones pinging against the windows. Hurricanes are fierce tropical spinning storms that can lift roofs, wrench trees from the ground and devastate a country. The centre of a hurricane is a much calmer area with lighter winds; this is called the **eye of the storm**. In different parts of the world, the hurricane has different names, such as:

typhoon   cyclone   willy-willy

Activity sheet – hurricanes

True or false?

Discuss the following statements. Decide whether each one is true or false.

Circle the correct answer

	Statement		
1.	A typhoon is another name for a hurricane.	True	False
2.	The eye of a hurricane is quite calm.	True	False
3.	Strong shelters can be built that will protect people from hurricanes.	True	False
4.	Changes in temperature between land and sea change the wind direction.	True	False
5.	During a hurricane, large objects may be picked up and hurled through the air.	True	False

Making questions

Can you change each of these statements into a question?

1. A typhoon is another name for a hurricane.

____

2. Hurricanes can wrench trees from the ground.

____

3. At sea, a hurricane whips up huge waves, endangering ships.

____

4. People who study the weather are **meteorologists**.

____

5. Hurricane names are given alphabetically and the first hurricane of the season begins with "A".

____

Activity 6: **Extreme winds – dictagloss**

This activity makes use of two short texts to develop pupils' listening skills.

Procedure

Working with ***Text One*** and ***Text Two*** that follow, use the same procedure as for Activity 1 in Part C above.

Text One: Cleaning up

Hurricanes leave a huge mess behind them. People who have been trapped in the wreckage have to be rescued. They need clean water, food, clothing and shelter. Some buildings might be partly standing but are unsafe. Disease can break out very quickly in these conditions. Stray animals need to be rounded up.

It can sometimes take years to rebuild cities after a hurricane.

Text Two: Tornadoes

The fiercest winds of all are those in a tornado. A tornado is a whirling funnel of air that is sometimes called a **twister**. A tornado is much smaller than a hurricane but it can pick up a building or a train and move it 50 metres away.

Tornadoes at sea are called **water-spouts**. Instead of sucking up trees and buildings, they suck up huge spouts of water.

Activity 7: **Extreme winds – hotseating**

Here the hotseat topic concerns tornadoes specifically.

Procedure

1. Choose a volunteer to sit in the hotseat. This child takes the role of someone who has just witnessed a tornado.
2. The other pupils ask questions to find out more about the experience. Here are some questions they could ask:
   - What did it sound like?
   - Was there any warning?
   - What happened?
   - How did you feel?
   - What did you do?

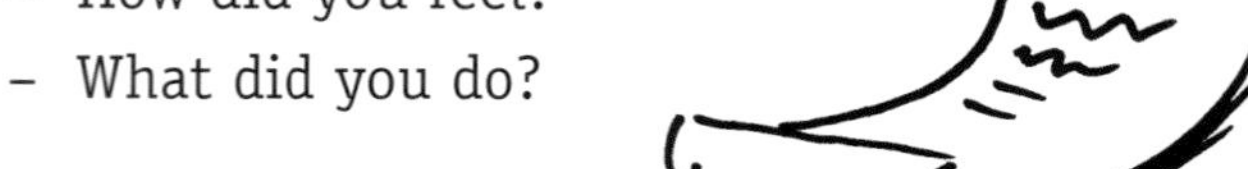

Activity 8: **Extreme winds – strategies for note taking**

This activity develops the pupils' skills in note taking by encouraging them to find the main ideas in a text.

Procedure

1. Give each child a copy of the ***air movement*** template (see Activity 5 above).
2. Re-read it as a class.
3. Discuss the main ideas together and highlight or underline them.

Activity 9: **Earthquakes – strategies for note taking**

This is another activity to develop the pupils' skills in note taking, this time focusing on earthquakes and a reading that is new to the class.

Procedure

1. Give out the ***earthquake task sheet*** that follows to each child.
2. Read through the instructions together. Tell them, "Find a partner. You have five minutes to discuss with your partner a good way to take notes on some information I will read to you. Work out what you will write down."
3. After the discussion in pairs, read the ***UK and San Francisco earthquakes*** article (which follows the template) to the children twice while they take notes about it.
4. All the children present their report on the earthquake to their partner, using their notes as the basis for the report.
5. Children complete the ***self assessment on note taking*** based on their experience
6. As a class, discuss the importance of being able to take relevant, useful notes. What strategies for taking notes worked well? Stress the importance of being able to identify key ideas in text.

Activity 10: **Emergency kits**

This activity involves a highly practical topic of discussion, which may motivate pupils and their families to prepare for an emergency.

Procedure

As a class, discuss which families have an emergency kit ready in the event of a natural disaster. What items would you need in such a kit?

Earthquake task sheet

- Work with a partner.
- You are going to listen to an article on earthquakes in the UK and San Francisco. Using the information in the article, you will then present your own report on the earthquakes. You will need to take notes. Discuss good strategies for taking notes.

Your notes

UK and San Francisco earthquakes

On Monday 23 September 2002, an earthquake measuring 4.8 on the Richter scale hit large parts of England and Wales. The tremor began at 12.53 am. Its epicentre was in Dudley in the West Midlands. Buildings shook for up to 30 seconds in parts of the West Midlands, Wales, North Yorkshire, London and Wiltshire. There was minor structural damage as homes were shaken, but no reports of any injuries. Aftershocks were felt later on Monday morning. This was the UK's largest earthquake for 10 years, although in world terms it would only classify as a light earthquake.

By contrast, an earthquake in California, USA on 18 April 1906 was one of the most significant earthquakes of all time. At 5.12 am a foreshock was felt widely throughout the San Francisco bay area. The great earthquake broke loose some 20 to 25 seconds later, with an epicentre near San Francisco. The strongest shaking lasted 45 to 60 seconds. It is estimated that the earthquake would have measured about 7.8 on the Richter scale. It was felt from southern Oregon to south of Los Angeles and inland as far as central Nevada. This earthquake is remembered most for the fire that followed it in San Francisco. That is why it is often known as the "San Francisco earthquake". At least 700 deaths were caused by the earthquake and fire. Most deaths were in San Francisco and 189 were reported elsewhere.

Self assessment on note taking

Circle the answer that shows what you think about your own skills in note taking.

I can listen to and identify key points.	Always	Sometimes	Not yet
I can read my notes.	Always	Sometimes	Not yet
I can take notes fast enough to keep up with the speaker.	Always	Sometimes	Not yet
I would be able to use my notes to write a report on the UK and San Francisco earthquakes.	Always	Sometimes	Not yet

Activity 11: **Volcanic eruptions**

Use this activity to establish some basic vocabulary and facts related to volcanic eruptions.

Procedure

1. Give a copy of the following ***volcano facts*** template to each pupil in the class.
2. Do the first part of the activity (discussing the vocabulary) as a class, then give the pupils time to work through the remaining questions on their own.

Activity 12: **Natural disasters ... three–two–one**

This final activity on natural disasters allows pupils to draw on all that they have learned about a particular topic.

Procedure

1. Each child chooses one of the following natural disasters as the topic of their speeches in this activity:

drought	flood	earthquake	tsunami
hurricane	volcanic eruption	avalanche	landslide

2. Organise the children into pairs.
3. One child in each pair has three minutes to speak to the other child on his or her chosen disaster.
4. After three minutes, you call, "Stop!" and then the second child in the pair speaks for three minutes on his or her own choice of disaster.
5. After another three minutes, you again call, "Stop!" and then children find a new partner. This time they have two minutes each to speak in their pairs on the same topic as last time.
6. By now the children are becoming more confident. They find a new partner and have one minute each to speak on their topic.

Hint

You can use the ***three–two–one peer assessment*** template in Section C, Activity 4 for assessment of the third and final speech.

Volcano facts

1. Read and discuss the vocabulary together.
2. Read and discuss the article "Boom!" together.
3. Use the vocabulary to help you complete the *true or false?* part of this activity.

Vocabulary

core	the solid centre of the Earth
crust	the outer layer of the Earth
mantle	the layer of the Earth between the core and the crust
extinct	a volcano that is no longer active
dormant	the condition of a sleeping volcano; it is going through a period of inactivity
lava	hot melted rock that has come out of the volcano
magma	hot melted rock that is below the Earth's surface.
volcanologist	a scientist who studies volcanoes

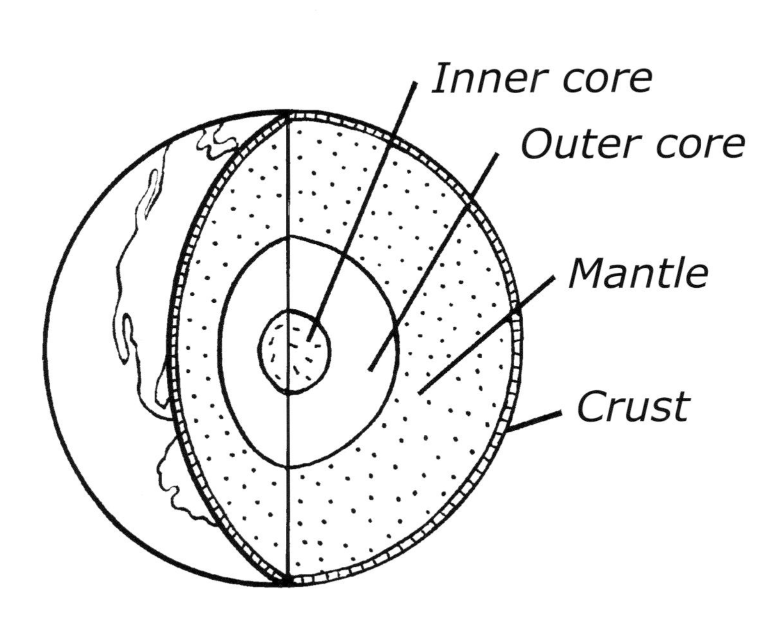

Boom!

The outer shell of the Earth, or the crust, is made up of slabs of rock. These slabs of rock are called plates. These plates can move and, as they move around, hot magma forces its way up to the surface between the plates. When the magma and hot gases force their way through the Earth's surface (or crust), there is an eruption and a volcano is formed.

In a large eruption, flows of lava down the mountain can wipe out properties and towns.

True or false?

Circle the correct answer for each statement.

1. The centre of the Earth is called the **core**. True False
2. A scientist who studies volcanoes is called a **meteorologist**. True False
3. The outer layer of the Earth is called the **crust**. True False
4. The layer between the core and the crust is called the **mantle**. True False
5. An **extinct** volcano is active. True False
6. An **extinct** volcano is no longer active. True False
7. A **dormant** volcano is extinct. True False
8. A **dormant** volcano is not extinct. True False
9. A volcano can erupt when hot magma rises up from the Earth's plates. True False
10. Lava flows from a volcano can cause a lot of damage. True False

F. Listening and responding to texts IV: Bonfire Night

This is the final set of activities that you can use as part of a curriculum study, or as a general knowledge component of your oral language programme. This topic deals with the historical background to Bonfire Night. Work with this topic for one or two weeks.

Activity 1: Before and after

This activity introduces the vocabulary and basic facts related to the Gunpowder Plot.

Procedure

1. Give each child a ***Bonfire Night vocabulary*** template.
2. Write *Bonfire Night* on the whiteboard and ask the children to write – in the *before* box on their template – all the words that they associate with Bonfire Night. They can work with a friend and share ideas if they wish.
3. Read about the ***Gunpowder Plot*** in the article that follows.
4. Ask the children to write – in the *after* box on their template – any new words that they now associate with Bonfire Night. Discuss any unfamiliar vocabulary such as *Protestant*.

Bonfire Night vocabulary

Before	After

The Gunpowder Plot

The Gunpowder Plot took place in 1605. James I was king of England and he was a Protestant. James wanted everyone in England to become Protestant and he made life very hard for the Catholics. They had to worship in secret and if they were caught they could be fined or imprisoned.

A group of Catholics led by a man called Robert Catesby made a plan to kill the king and his parliament. Guy Fawkes was asked to help because of his knowledge of gunpowder.

First the men decided to dig a tunnel under the Houses of Parliament so that, when the parliament was meeting there, they could blow it up. Guy rented the house next door and moved in there. While they were digging, they discovered a cellar under the Houses of Parliament and they hid 36 barrels of gunpowder in the cellar.

Unfortunately for Guy, one of the lords of parliament received an anonymous letter warning him not to attend the meeting. The king was told and the cellar was searched. Guy was captured and tortured to try to get him to tell the names of the others in the plot. The plotters were rounded up and either killed or put in the Tower of London. Each year on 5 November people celebrate the failure of the Gunpowder Plot with fireworks and bonfires. People today still sometimes make "Guys" and burn them on a bonfire.

In many countries there are restrictions on the sale of fireworks for safety reasons.

Activity 2: **Story grid**

The following story grid offers a set of vocabulary related to the Gunpowder Plot, as a loose guide to writing a story about it.

Procedure

1. Give each child a copy of the following ***Gunpowder Plot story grid***.
2. The children write the story of Guy Fawkes, using all the words on the grid.

Extension

Hold a class debate on the topic: "That fireworks should be banned". (See more on debating in Book 2 of *Speaking in Sentences*.)

Gunpowder Plot story grid

King James	Catholic	Protestant	parliament
Robert Catesby	tunnel	cellar	gunpowder
Guy Fawkes	plot	tortured	fireworks

G. Ten-minute teasers

Here are some quick activities for filling up a brief amount of time with some good learning experiences.

Activity 1: What happened?

Procedure

1. Choose one of the following exclamations and say it to the class:

Ouch!	Thank you!	Help!	Hurry, please!
No!	Come here!	I don't believe it!	Go away!
Call an ambulance!	Police!		

2. Challenge the class to tell you what happened in the time leading up to the exclamation. What provoked it?

Activity 2: Word tennis

This activity was provided by Keren Wallace.

Procedure

1. Choose two children to stand in front of the class. Give these two children a topic and say which of them is going to start.
2. The two children take turns to say a word that is associated with the topic. If one of them pauses for longer than three seconds or repeats a word that has already been said, he or she is out.
3. Choose another child to challenge the winner of the first round.
4. Continue in this way for as long as time and attention spans allow.

Activity 3: The language of speech

Procedure

1. Give out a copy of the following ***language effects*** template to each child.
2. Choose one or two language effects from the template to discuss with the children, check their understanding and do the follow up tasks.

Language effects

Language effect	Example(s)	Follow up
Exaggeration (overstating)	*I sold my stereo and made a fortune.*	When do we exaggerate? Why do we exaggerate? Think of examples.
Understatement	*I guess I did all right in the test. I got 80%.*	Can you think of more examples?
Contrast (juxtaposition) – positive and negative concepts or language are side by side	*You have spoilt all your good work.*	Can you think of more examples?
Alliteration – repeating the initial letter in a phrase or sentence; often used in tongue twisters	*Granny's grumpy gardener …* *Catherine's coconut cookies …*	Make up some tongue twisters of your own.
Rhetorical questions – questions that usually don't require an answer	*Are you sure about that? I don't agree…* *You really like that don't you?*	Listen for rhetorical questions in everyday conversation.
Onomatopoeia – words that sound like the noun or action being described	*squelch* *moo* *rustle* *crackle*	Make up some onomatopoeic words of your own.
Personification – giving human characteristics to something that is not human	*The outboard motor coughed.* *The engine roared into life.*	What are some more examples?
Simile – comparing one object to another using *like* or *as*	*He ran like the wind.* *She felt as cold as ice.*	Read a story and look for similes.
Metaphor – identifying one thing as another; comparing aspects of two unrelated things	*She is a tower of strength.* *He had an icy gaze.*	Read a story and look for metaphors.

SECTION TWO

Intensives

This section contains a range of ideas particularly for working with a group of children with special oral language needs.

A. Using school announcements

Use the announcement system in your school to build up children's self-confidence.

Ideas

- Ask if a child from the group could give a news bulletin before lunch. If a child has produced a worthwhile poem or short piece of writing, let him or her use this time to read it to the school.
- When the "sit-down for lunch" period is over, ask a child to give the instructions about clearing up rubbish and to tell the others to go to "play".

B. Predicting language

Activity: Words for pictures

Procedure

1. Give a copy of the ***what are they saying?*** template that follows to each child.
2. Work through the template together.

Extension

- The children watch a DVD, or part of a DVD, with the sound turned off.
- Regularly stop the DVD and ask the children to guess what the characters have been saying.

C. Storytelling

Activity: **Once upon a time**

This activity is concerned with retelling traditional tales.

Procedure

1. Choose a traditional tale to read to the group.
2. Photocopy some of the pictures that accompany the story.
3. Ask a child to re-tell the story. Use the pictures as flash cards or prompts as the child is re-telling it.

Extension

- Show the children a picture of a natural disaster such as a volcano erupting or a flood. Discuss the effect of the disaster on the surrounding community.
- Tell a story (true or imaginary) about a natural disaster.
- Make a display of pictures. Caption the pictures and build up a word bank.

D. Listening and responding to texts

Each activity in this section starts from a text from which one or more tasks are built. Topics covered by the texts are:

1. penguins
2. searching for oil
3. marine mammals
4. waterways.

Activity 1: **Penguins**

Procedure

1. Give a copy of the ***penguin worksheet*** that follows to each child.
2. Tell the children that you are going to read them an article about penguins and they will note down its main ideas in the top part of the worksheet.
3. Read the ***penguins*** article that follows, while the pupils take notes.
4. Give each child a copy of the ***penguins*** article.
5. Go through the text together and highlight or underline the main ideas.
6. Read the following statements to the children. For each statement, they write *T* or *F* for the *true or false?* task on their worksheet.

   (a) All penguins live in hot areas.
   (b) They like to swim in the sea.
   (c) They lay two to four eggs.
   (d) Penguins are good parents.
   (e) Fish is the main food of penguins.
   (f) Penguins live in Antarctica.

What are they saying?

Jack is introducing his mother to his new teacher. What is he saying?

Jack is showing his new puppy to his friend. What is he saying?

Jack is ringing his friend to ask him if he can come to stay for the weekend. What is he saying?

Jack was late for school today. What is he saying to the teacher?

The football coach is talking to the team before its game begins. What is he saying?

Penguins

Many penguins live amongst snow and ice. Some penguins live in Antarctica, where no plants grow so there is little shelter from blizzards and snowfalls. Penguins playfully slide down snow-banks. In the sea they catch fish to eat.

When a mother penguin lays her egg, she cannot make a nest, so she keeps the egg on her feet and snuggled against her body to keep it warm. When the mother goes hunting for food, the father looks after the egg.

By the time the baby penguin hatches from the egg, light is returning to Antarctica.

Penguin worksheet

Facts about penguins

____

____

____

____

____

____

____

____

True or false?

Write T or F beside each letter.

(a)	(c)	(e)
(b)	(d)	(f)

Activity 2: **Oil**

Procedure

1. Give a copy of the ***oil worksheet*** that follows to each child.
2. Tell the children that you are going to read them an article called "Searching for oil" and their task is to note the main ideas in the top part of the worksheet.
3. Read them the ***searching for oil*** article that follows, while the children take notes.
4. Give the children a copy of the ***searching for oil*** article. Read the article through together, highlighting or underlining the main points.
5. Carry out the experiment on the worksheet and record what happens.
6. Conduct a three–two–one activity in which children speak with a partner on the topic of oil. With the first partner, they have three minutes each in which to speak; with the second partner they have two minutes; with the third partner they have one minute. (For more on the three–two–one procedure, see Section One, Part C, Activity 4.)

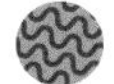

Extension

The children investigate why the price of petrol changes so much.

Activity 3: **Marine mammals**

Procedure

1. Start a dictagloss session by asking the children to find a partner.
2. Tell the children, "You are going to listen to a short piece of writing. You will need to focus on the key ideas and see if you can remember all the important points. You need to remember because you are going to re-tell the story to your partner."
3. Choose one of the paragraphs from the ***mammals*** article and read the text twice.
4. While you are reading the text for the second time, write some key words on the whiteboard.
5. When you have finished reading the first text, one child re-tells the story to his or her partner.
6. The pupil who is telling the story asks, "Can you think of anything else?" and the listening pupil attempts to fill in any gaps.
7. The whole class tries to re-tell the text. Write the class version on the whiteboard and compare it to the original. Are all the main ideas there?
8. Choose a second paragraph from the ***mammals*** article and read it while the children reverse roles.
9. Discuss the following questions.
   - People are warm-blooded. What does this mean?
   - What are two other characteristics of mammals?
   - If an animal is extinct, what has happened?
   - What is the largest animal that ever lived?
   - What do you know about the bottle-nosed dolphin?
   - Which marine animals are sometimes known as the wolves of the sea? Why?

Searching for oil

Why do we need oil?

Lorries, cars, aeroplanes, ships ... almost all means of transport use oil. Many companies are constantly searching for oil to be made into petrol.

Oil is used to keep machines running smoothly and to help generate electric power. It is combined with chemicals to produce synthetics such as plastics, nylon and polythene.

Where is oil found?

Oil is found deep in the earth between layers of hard rock. Decayed plants and animals, air and water that have been trapped together for a long time turn into oil.

Scientists called geologists are always looking for sites, drilling and taking samples of rock to test, in case the area contains oil. Huge amounts of money are spent on drilling exploratory wells.

Dynamite is used to blast the rocks. At sea, oil rigs are constructed and used to support all the necessary equipment. Divers, engineers, electricians, boats and helicopters are all needed. In shallow water, floating rigs can be firmly anchored to sea beds. The hardest place to drill for oil is in deep water. Workers stay on the rigs for weeks at a time. They work in shifts to share their duties across 24 hours each day; during their time off they sleep, work, or read and watch films. When oil is struck, the oil and gas escape up the borehole and spurt into the air.

Occasionally there are accidents that result in oil spills at sea. The oil floats on the sea, forming dark patches. These patches are called oil slicks and they are a danger to fish and bird life. Oil coats the feathers of the sea birds and they cannot fly. Plants around the shoreline also die.

Fortunately these accidents do not happen often.

Oil worksheet

Searching for oil – key ideas

Experiment

1. Add some oil to a bottle that has been half-filled with water.

   What happens?

2. Shake the bottle and then let it stand.

   What happens?

3. Now add some washing-up liquid to the bottle and shake it again.

   What happens?

Mammals

What is a mammal?

Mammals live on land, at sea, in the air and under the ground. A mammal is warm-blooded. People are mammals. Mammals have fur or hair on their body. Most mammals do not lay eggs; they give birth to live babies. Mammals feed their young on milk.

Bottle-nosed dolphin

Bottle-nosed dolphins are intelligent and curious mammals. They are sometimes used in aquarium shows and like to follow fishing boats at sea. They have a dark grey back with lighter grey sides and live in the shallower water near the shore.

Blue whale

The blue whale is the largest animal that ever lived; it is even bigger than dinosaurs. It can weigh up to 200 tonnes and lives on tiny sea creatures called krill. It does not attack people. This whale was nearly hunted to extinction and there are far fewer whales in the world's oceans than there used to be.

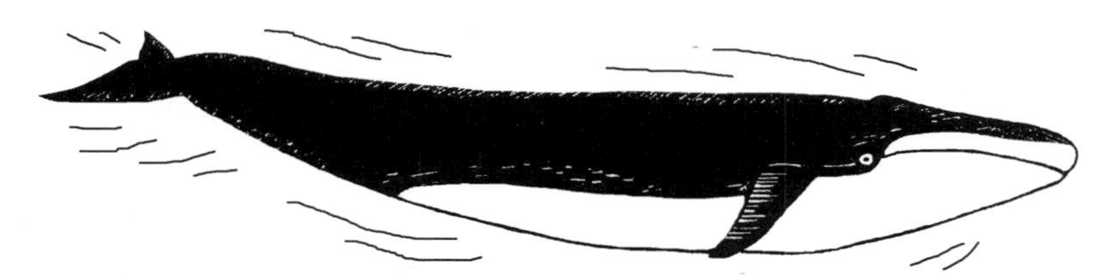

Killer whale (orca)

Killer whales hunt in packs and are sometimes known as the wolves of the sea. They have about 40 sharp teeth, but the shape of their teeth means that they cannot chew their food. They take large bites of their prey and swallow them whole. They have been known to attack blue whales but usually hunt seals and dolphins. There are no records of humans being attacked by killer whales. They grow up to approximately 10 metres long.

Activity 4: **Waterways**

Procedure

1. Give a copy of the ***waterways worksheet*** that follows to each child.
2. Read the ***waterways*** article to the children while they tick each word at the top of the worksheet as they hear it.
3. Discuss the meanings of the words on the worksheet.
4. The children write a poem or story about a river. For example, they might begin:

   At the top of a hill was a tiny spring
   It trickled down
   Between the clumps of grass
   Over stones

Extension

- Give a copy of the ***waterways*** article to each pupil and they underline the words listed on their worksheet.

Waterways

How does a river system work?

Where does the water come from? Where does it go?

A river system is made up of a river and all the water that flows into it. The water comes from springs, from creeks that flow into the river, from rain and from melting snow.

The area of land drained by the river system is called the **river catchment**. Water from rain and melting snow collects in puddles. Some of the water seeps into the ground and is known as ground water. This water moves downhill through the ground until it reaches the lowest point or until it reaches a layer of rock that is impermeable, which means that water cannot pass through it. A spring forms when **ground water** makes its way back to the surface, then trickles downhill until it reaches a stream or creek. Rivers flow downhill to the lowest point and usually end up at the sea.

Change in the river

Water levels rise and fall quite quickly depending on the amount of rain and melting snow. Cutting down trees can make the water flow more quickly off the land.

Earthquakes can change the course of a river. People build dams and alter the river's course.

Reference: Ministry of Education (NZ). Building Science Concepts. Waterways.

Waterways worksheet

Can you hear these words?

Ground water

Impermeable

River catchment

Flow

Course

Seeps

The story of a river

E. Listening, responding and describing

These two activities will actively engage pupils with a particular topic and encourage them to extend their own descriptive skills.

Activity 1: Grasshopper

Procedure

1. If possible, have a live grasshopper for the children to observe. Otherwise, have plenty of pictures for them to look at.
2. Give a copy of the ***grasshopper worksheet*** that follows to each child. The children write as many relevant words as they can think of around the picture of the grasshopper. Help their thinking with incomplete statements such as:

   A grasshopper has ...

   A grasshopper can ...
3. Revise nouns. Which of the words that the children have written are nouns? Make a list on the whiteboard.
4. Revise verbs and then adjectives in a similar way.
5. Introduce comparative adjectives, such as *bigger*, and use them in context to ask questions:

   What insects are bigger (or smaller) than a grasshopper?
6. Choose three or four children and give each child one minute to describe a grasshopper or some other insect to the group.

Activity 2: Cockerel

1. Give a copy of the ***cockerel worksheet*** that follows to each child. The children to write as many relevant words as they can think of around the picture of the cockerel. Help their thinking with incomplete statements such as:

   A cockerel has ...

   A cockerel can ...
2. Revise nouns. Which of the words that the children have written are nouns? Make a list on the whiteboard. Introduce new vocabulary such as *comb*.
3. Revise verbs and adjectives in the same way.
4. Introduce comparative adjectives, such as *bigger*, and use them in context to ask questions:

   What birds are bigger (or smaller) than a cockerel?
5. Choose three or four children and give each child one minute to describe a cockerel to the group.

Grasshopper worksheet

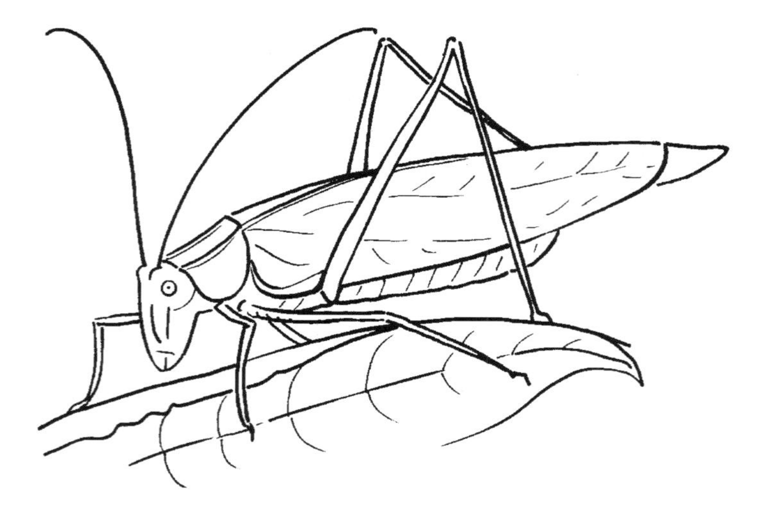

Cockerel worksheet

One-year oral language programmes with the *Speaking in Sentences* series

Years 1–4

Autumn term			
Week 1	News* Story starters, Book 1, Part 2	Weeks 7–8	News Using pronouns, Book 1, Part 4
Week 2	News Re-telling stories, Book 1, Part 2	Weeks 9–10	News Sequence stories, Book 1, Part 5
Week 3	News Describing in the negative, Book 1, Part 2	Week 11	News* Introducing and interviewing a speaker, Book 1, Part 2
Week 4	News Expanding vocabulary, Book 1, Part 2 I Spy, Book 1, Part 2	Weeks 12–14	News Barrier games, Book 1, Part 6
Weeks 5–6	News Comprehension and related activities, Book 1, Part 3	Week 15	News Impromptu speeches, Book 1, Part 2

* Have news on Monday each week (see doughnut news, Book 4, Section One, Part A).

Years 1–4 continued

Spring term			
Weeks 1–2	News Guessing from an estimation jar, Book 2, Part 1 Rhyming bag, Book 2, Part 1	Weeks 7–9	News and more Using masks and puppets, Book 2, Part 1
Week 3	News Memories, Book 2, Part 1	Week 10	News and more Giving instructions and following instructions, Book 2, Part 1
Week 4	News Object identification table, Book 2, Part 1	Weeks 11–12	News and more Cooking, Book 2, Part 1
Weeks 5–6	News and more** More ideas for barrier games, Book 2, Part 3		

Summer term			
Week 1	News and more Cooking, Book 2, Part 1	Week 8	News and more Conversation – what can you see? (questioning skills), Book 1, Part 4 Charades, Book 3, Section Two, Part G
Week 2	News and more Rub-out technique, Book 2, Part 1	Week 9	News and more Using positional vocabulary, Book 2, Part 1 Identifying objects and their function, Book 2, Part 1
Weeks 3–5	News and more** Bookselling, Book 3, Section One, Part J	Week 10	News and more Impromptu speeches, Book 1, Part 2
Week 6	News and more Talking and asking questions about pictures, Book 2, Part 1 Hide the object, Book 1, Part 2	Weeks 11–12	News and more More reading aloud, Book 3, Section One, Part D
Week 7	News and more Talking and asking questions about pictures, Book 2, Part 1 Conversation – what would you like? (questioning skills), Book 1, Part 3		

** Continue with doughnut news each Monday but begin to phase in more structured challenges. See "Moving on from news" (Book 4, Section One, Part A).

Years 5–6

Autumn term			
Week 1	News about the holidays	Weeks 4–7	Bookselling, Book 3, Section One, Part J
Week 2	Charades (questioning skills), Book 3, Section Two, Part G	Weeks 8–10	Barrier games, Books 1 and 2
Week 3	Using pronouns, Book 1, Part 4, Activities 3–6	Weeks 11–15	Storytelling: select from activities in Book 4, Section One, Part B and Section Two, Part C
Spring term			
Weeks 1–4	Following and giving instructions, Book 3, Section Two, Part J	Weeks 9–11	More reading aloud, Book 3, Section One, Part D
Weeks 5–6	Impromptu speeches, Book 1, Part 2	Week 12	Presenting poems with partners, Book 3, Section One, Part B
Weeks 7–8	Preparing speeches, Book 2, Part 4		
Summer term			
Week 1	Presenting poems with partners, Book 3, Section One, Part B	Weeks 7–8	Dialogues with two people, Book 3, Section One, Part K
Week 2	Using positional vocabulary, Book 2, Part 1	Week 9	Descriptive language – word imaging, Book 2, Part 1 Dictagloss, Book 4, Section One, Parts C–F
Week 3	Word tennis, Book 4, Section One, Part G	Weeks 10–12	Dictagloss, Book 4, Section One, Parts C–F
Weeks 4–6	Listening, responding and describing, Book 4, Section Two, Part E		

Years 7–8

Autumn term			
Week 1	Communication, Book 3, Section One, Part A	Week 7	Word tennis, Book 4, Section One, Part G
Weeks 2–4	Presenting poems with partners, Book 3, Section One, Part B	Weeks 8–10	Storytelling: select from activities in Book 4, Section One, Part B and Section Two, Part C
Weeks 5–6	Dialogues with two people, Book 3, Section One, Part K	Weeks 11–15	Focus on using visual texts to stimulate oral language this term, Book 3, Section One, Parts E–I and Section Two, Parts A–C
Spring term (speech making as focus)			
Weeks 1–2	Revise and extend use of visual texts from autumn term	Weeks 9–10	An introduction to debating, Book 2, Part Five
Weeks 3–4	Impromptu speeches, Book 1, Part Two	Week 11	Charades, Book 3, Section Two, Part G
Weeks 5–6	Making speeches to inform ..., Book 3, Section One, Part L	Week 12	Word tennis, Book 4, Section One, Part G
Weeks 7–8	Making speeches ... for special occasions, Book 3, Section One, Part L		
Summer term			
Weeks 1–12	Focus on listening and responding to texts this term, Book 4, Section One, Parts C–F		